An Open Heart
The journey of an overachiever

JESUS EMMANUEL ORIGEL

An Open Heart

Copyright © 2020 by Jesus Emmanuel Origel. All rights reserved.

No part of this publication may be reproduced, stored in a retrieval system or transmitted in any way by any means, electronic, mechanical, photocopy, recording or otherwise without the prior permission of the author except as provided by USA copyright law.

The opinions expressed by the author are not necessarily those of URLink Print and Media.

1603 Capitol Ave., Suite 310 Cheyenne, Wyoming USA 82001
1-888-980-6523 | admin@urlinkpublishing.com

URLink Print and Media is committed to excellence in the publishing industry.

Book design copyright © 2020 by URLink Print and Media. All rights reserved.

Published in the United States of America
ISBN 978-1-64753-361-8 (Paperback)
ISBN 978-1-64753-362-5 (Digital)

01.05.20

An Open Heart

Contents

Acknowledgments 9
Dedication 11
Preface 13
Introduction 15
The Underdogs 17
Life of Worries 18
Emotional Sorrow 19
I Cry 20
To My Unknown Love 21
Preparation for My Death 22
A Torn Heart 23
Under the Skies of Heaven 24
A Heart of a Lion 25
A Rose that Grew as a "Second" 26
My Life 27
Maturity and Wisdom 28
The Pride of a Chicano 29
My Best Friend 30
Corruption 31
When I Die 32
If I Must Die 33
How to Remember Me 34
We All Die 35
Two Portions of My Soul 36
My Legacy 37
My Father's Wisdom 38
The Pride of an Emigrate Father 39

My City	40
Stressful Days and Worrisome Nights	41
A Letter to My Estranged Family Member	42
All the Drama in My Life	43
Praise All Women	44
Friends Come and Go	45
Reason I Write	46
Is This Really Life?	47
The Savior of My Life	48
Life Is a Trip	49
The Ultimate Educator	50
Where Did I Go Wrong?	51
In My Realm of Loneliness	52
I Cry Inside	53
Uncertain Future	54
My Bed	55
My Prayer	56
Love Is One of a Kind	57
Life Is a Book	58
An End of an Era	59
It's Me	60
Scares of Sorrow	61
Remember Me	62
A Call to All Chicanos	63
To All My Readers	64
God Bless the Dead	65
Your Voice	66
Life Is a Risk	67
Those We Loved and Lost, RIP	68
Thank You, Mom	69
My Time to Shine	70
Origel	71
Many Mountains to Climb	72
My Birth	73

I'm Here	74
Book of a Dream	75
Family Tree	76
In My Shell	77
The Hourglass	78
Power of Desire	79
The Thoughts of a Crazy Individual	80
Revolutionaries of the Past	81
About the Author	89
About the Book	91

Acknowledgments

This opportunity means a great deal to me to continue pursuing my artistic creative writing ambitions goals and dreams. Therefore, I would like to thank URL ink Publishing Company for working with me throughout this process. Furthermore, I'm truly grateful towards every one who believed in me and my potential even when I failed to see it for myself.

Most of all, I send a thank you to all my readers and supporters. Since I was born and raised in Oceanside, California, many individuals have impacted my life. Regardless of whether you moved away, we are not in contact, or my memories of you are negative or positive, I owe you a thank you. I also thank my compadres who passed away, the ones I still communicate with, and those who still live here in Oceanside. And to my friends around the world, who I consider part of my extended family, I appreciate you all.

I can't forget all my family friends, who treated me so kindly. I owe a special thank you to all my family members all over the world. And especially my own family, including all my uncles, aunts, and cousins. Most of all, my immediate family members—my two beautiful sisters, my brothers-in-law, and my nephews—I love you all. My sisters, I thank you for being highly educated, which drove me to further my education. When I was younger, I found my sister poetry and was inspired to write my thoughts into poetry. My other sister is so intelligent, which further inspired me to achieve my professional dreams. My sisters made my parents extremely proud of them, which made me strive to make my parents proud of me. I am further inspired by all of my four adorable nephews. I'm so proud of each and every one of them.

My father instilled a strong work ethic within me to become determined and to persist in achieving my goals. My mother words can't describe the love I have for my mother. Nor can I begin to mention all she means to my life.

Dedication

To my father, and my mother. Most especially my father's parents.
Most important, my mother's parents, whom passed away a few years ago.

Preface

My family history is very important to me. My parents migrated from Mexico in 1971, in search for a better life. But, struggles and disadvantages were not far behind. I was greatly affected by all the difficulties my parents had to endure. Both of my parents are from the beautiful state of Michoacán, home of the Purépecha indigenous people, which made me prouder and more interested in my heritage. My father is very proud of his ethnicity, and he instilled that in all his children. My father was born in Morelia, Michoacán, Mexico. These are my family roots, which continue to shape my life. To be able to write this book is an honor and privilege. I always wanted to write a book about my life, to leave a lasting impact on this world. Also, to touch people in order to inspire and motivation others to reach their full potential within their own life. This book is meant to be focused on spreading a message of hope.

Introduction

On September 14, 1986, I was born, a premature birth. I spent the first two weeks of my life in the hospital fighting for my life. Before the age of five years old, I had already undergone two surgeries. Because of my premature birth and two surgeries, I suffered many setbacks and disadvantages.

I also witnessed and heard many things that shaped my life. This book was written throughout my life as a way to pour out my soul and get all my feelings off my chest in a way that might be useful to others. It is also a way to pass my wisdom to future generations, who will change the world.

This is a collection of my thoughts and words of encouragement. This book is an attempt to tell my life story and relate to others in order to inspire and motivate them to chase their own goals and dreams regardless of the obstacles that life brings.

But again, I must clarify this book and my writings within this book is less about me as the author and more about the message of hope.

My Thoughts on Death

Since an adolescent age
I had experienced the deaths
Of near and dear individuals.
Their deaths left lasting effects on my life.
People are born,
They live, and then die.
That's a part of life.
What can you do? It's true.
Just hope they lived the best lives they could.
But sadly, most don't.
Just hope and pray for them
To enter a better place called heaven.

The Underdogs

To the underdogs—
They are few
But lost and forgotten
By many.
Their struggles are far and wide.
Some were left behind,
But now it's their time to shine.
So stand tall,
And reach for the sky.
Never let your dreams die.
Long live the underdogs.

Life of Worries

Life is full of worries
That bring stress.
I must confess
My life is a mess.
I'm in complete distress.
Life must be a test.
I hope I get everything off of my chest
Before I get put to rest.

Emotional Sorrow

Sometimes I cry with no one to ask why.
Sometimes I cry when I'm alone.
I cry because I'm on my own with my thoughts.
The tears I shed are bittersweet.
They flow like leaves falling from a tree.
My tears are slow but take the form of many.
The world moves on with no end in sight,
With a fast pace and blind at times.
A too-fast world would much rather pass you by
Then stop and ask why you cry.
It hurts so bad; that makes me sad
And a bit mad to know no one cares
To fully understand my emotional sorrow.

I Cry

I cry because my heart is torn.
Sometimes it is hard to carry on.
I wish I had an ear to confide in
And a shoulder to cry on.
But since I don't,
I'm left to stand on my own
With no one to ask
Why I cry.

To My Unknown Love

My future love,
With you in my life, it fills me with warmth.
You are the apple of my eye.
For you—I will always try to fill you with joy
And be the best man I can for you.
Just treat me right, and trust in me;
I won't let you down.
I will make sure our future will be bright,
Like a star in the night sky.
In my eyes, I dream to tuck you in every night
With a goodnight kiss.
To send you sweet dreams
And send you off to dreamland nice and tight.

In my soul I burn with the desire to hug you
With all my might and never let you go.
My love, when I see you, my heart
Beats so fast and violently,
Like a blast from a gun
In the middle of a lonely forest.
This is only the beginning
Of the meaning you bring to my life.

Preparation for My Death

I can't understand the fear of death.
Why are people so afraid of death?
People know death is coming, yet still fear it.
And they fail to see death for what it means,
Not what it is; therefore,
Everyone seems to fear it, but not I.
I only fear my readiness for my death.
My preparation for my death is
My design for my whole life.
So, my life is in preparation for my death.

A Torn Heart

I was always alone.
I chose to be alone.
I'm alone with my deep thoughts.
My soul is like an endless fire
That burns so bright
The flames touch the sky.
The flames are so hot
They will tear any heart apart.
But who will fully understand?
Why my heart is torn?
That is the question
With so many answers
To a torn heart.

Under the Skies of Heaven

Long-lost love,
But never forgotten,
You are somewhere above
While I wait anxiously
For you to bless me
With your love.
How I wish you were here.
But you will always be
Near and dear to my heart
And set it apart.

A Heart of a Lion

My heart is that of a lion.
Its roar is loud and strong.
My heart is never satisfied
With one's position
And craves more.
My heart is heavy and big
From my drive and determination
That keeps me persisting.
My heart is full of self-pride,
Like a lion in a jungle.
Yet my soul is that of a teddy bear,
With the emotion of a broken heart.
This combination of feelings
Makes it difficult to sleep.
That's the price I pay
For a heart of a lion.

A Rose that Grew as a "Second"

A rose that bloomed in a field of firsts.
Did you hear about the rose?
That was almost thrown away
Like it was cured?
It was frail and fragile
But blossomed
From the category of "seconds."
What a sight to see.
So long live all the
Roses called "seconds."
A rose like no other,
Beautiful and strong.
Yet few cares to see.

My Life

Take a walk in my shoes.
Feel the pain in my heart.
Feel all the conflicts in my soul.
Take a seat in the car.
Travel down the road called my life.
Look in my eyes,
So, you see what I see.
Hear what I hear,
And feel what I feel.
Then and only then
Will you fully understand me?
Until then, don't judge me.
Only God can judge me.
God knows I try
To find my complete, everlasting happiness.
That's why I cry internally.
This is my life.

Maturity and Wisdom

Maturity and wisdom are very important.
They belong together, like a man and a woman.
They also play major roles in evolution.
They allow a boy to become a man
And a girl become a woman.
Since maturity and wisdom come
With age and experience,
They take the form of many subjects
And are taught by virtually everyone.
One without the other
Leads you to become ignorant.
Ignorance can be deadly.
Sadly, so many people
Choose to live with hate in their hearts
Due to their lack of
Maturity and wisdom.

The Pride of a Chicano

The pride of a Chicano
Is as long as it is wide.
Roots are deep,
And their history is
Lost but never eased.
Their struggle is continuous.
This is the weight they carry
Like chips on their shoulders
And pains in our hearts.
This must never be forgotten,
The pride of a Chicano.

My Best Friend

Our connection grew from the start.
Soon, our connection was
Meaningful and deep.
You were my best friend—
The only one I could lean on.
The only one I could confide in,
One I could count on not
To judge or misunderstand me.
My only friend at the time.
With you I felt comfort.
Even though you were man's best friend,
You made me feel special.
And for that, our connection
Was judged and misunderstood.
You were my best friend until the end.
My only friend multiped by ten.
But just like that,
It was done.

Corruption

Corruption affects us all.
With its tentacles, it touches us all
Until we fall.
It reaches and takes
Our minds, bodies, and souls.
For some, even in whole.
It is the cancer in us all.
It spreads and spreads.
Why must you doom us all?
Are we that poor in faith?
For you to lead us astray,
While your fest is our pray
With no end in sight
To your evil ways?

When I Die

When I die,
I want to be loved by many
And known by many.
Feared by none
While being respected by all.
I know I'll be forgotten by some.
Just know I'm a survivor.
Don't cry when I die.
Just know I'm finally free.
God, please forgive me.
Allow the sky to open for me.
Allow the star to be bright
To guide my soul like a light.

Like my life that used to
Hold me so tight,
Now she lets me go.
So, don't cry.
Just keep my legacy alive,
Especially in the minds and eyes
That will profit from my demise.

If I Must Die

So, I say goodbye
In the event of my demise.
For all the pain in my heart
And all the hurt in my eyes
There is no more.
My stress is over.
I just hope this will help you cope.
You will always be
In my heart and prayers.
I now found peace of mind.
I will happily give up my life
In hope of saving yours.
So, rest assured,
I want the best for all of you.
I hope my task is complete
Before my time has passed.
The end is near.
I pray I did something
For you to remember.

How to Remember Me

Remember me how I lived,
Not how I died.
Choose to remember me
With good thoughts,
For I played my hand
Like a poker player.
Now it is time for me to go.
I say, "*Ciao* for now."
Hope you don't mourn for me.
Just learn from me,
And learn how to remember me.

We All Die

Why must we live to die?
We all must die
So, our souls can fly
Up high
To the sky
In order to meet
our Creator.

Two Portions of My Soul

There are two portions of my soul,
Like a bird on each shoulder
Pulling me apart.
One is a young, while the other is older at heart.
One is a boy, while the other is a man.
This battle is difficult to withstand.
People fail to understand
The beauty within this duo.
Where my individuality lies
Tatted on my chest
In remembrance
To remain truthful
To the two portions of my soul.

My Legacy

My legacy I leave behind.
My life's journey was not always kind.
Nevertheless, it was mine.
In redemption I find
Peace of mind
In the words I spoke
And the path I took.
But is that enough
To be read like a book
And not be judged
By some immature actions I took?

My Father's Wisdom

I'm my father's son,
The keeper of his wisdom,
The carrier of his legacy,
The holder of his knowledge,
His only son.
The greatest life lessons—
Those of a father to his son.

The Pride of an Emigrate Father

The pride of an emigrate father
Is long and difficult to understand.
Yet special and unique,
Full of love and life lessons
Stemming from struggles of his past
And history of his motherland.

My City

The city I love,
The city embedded on my chest
And in my heart,
Is pulling me apart.
The city is not the same.
Changing at a fast pace,
Too fast and different
To recognize
With my own two eyes.
But where the beauty lies,
I tell no lies.
This is my city.
I'm a product of this community.
This is my home,
Where I was born and raised
In my city.

Stressful Days and Worrisome Nights

My days are full of stress.
My nights are worrisome.
Difficult to find peace in my mind,
Which is like a runaway train
That never stops or brakes.
My soul strives for time to rest.
I guess life is a test.
All I can do is my best
And hope I get everything off of my chest.

A Letter to My Estranged Family Member

Life is like a roller coaster,
With all its ups and downs.
And no family is perfect,
So we need to forgive and move on as a family.
The bond of family is strong and lasts longer than any friendship
Because family is a blood connection, not water,
Even though I didn't always show my love for you.
My love for you is like a cake—
Big and beautiful but hard to handle at times,
No matter how hard one might try to replicate.

All the Drama in My Life

Drama—seems like it overfills my life like water.
Drama has always been a part of my life.
At times I miss it, so I seek it.
Throughout my life, I can't seem to fully escape all the drama that surrounds me.
I guess that's why people say, "Life goes on, and the world stops for no one."
I was born into drama; I grew up expecting it,
Like a mother expecting her unborn child.
My drama seems to come from every angle.
But as I grew up and became a man,
I learned how to cope and deal with it and adapt.

Praise All Women

Remember, you are precious.
You are strong and brave,
Such beautiful and intelligent
Human beings with hearts of gold
Who carry new life into the world?
Bless all women
For they raise the future
That lights the minds,
That ushers in great change.
So, praise all women.

Friends Come and Go

Friends come in different forms.
People are quick to judge another's actions.
But who will care to understand why you acted in that matter?
And who can you count on to listen when you need a shoulder to cry on?
Friends are a dime a dozen.
Friends come and go.
But true friends are hard to find,
So, treasure them with all your heart.
Sadly, friends go their separate ways.
Friendships are like fame,
Based on popularity and convenience,
But not a necessity to have.
If not chosen wisely and properly maintained,
It can bring you to a messy end.

Reason I Write

My thoughts flow
Onto the paper
With ease,
Like the ocean
With its cool breeze.
Many feelings are in my mind.
So please
Let my voice be heard
With ease.

Is This Really Life?

Is this how it is supposed to be?
Why must only the strong survive
And thrive,
While others take a dive?
Is this really life?
This can't be my true life
While the spirit is
Crying out
For life.

The Savior of My Life

With her gentle touch,
She warms my heart.
Her voice
Claims my soul.
Her heart shows me
Unconditional love.
In her beautiful eyes,
I find comfort.
Her prayers
Give me light
To fight.

Life Is a Trip

This life is full of highs and lows.
Full of many bumpy roads
With many obstacles
To undergo.
But it's your life,
So, don't let go.
Hang on for dear life.

The Ultimate Educator

Life is your best teacher,
And you are a constant pupil.
No escaping.
The wheels of your mind
Keep turning.
You are in an ever-growing state
Of learning
While your life story is hurting
To be told.

Where Did I Go Wrong?

There is something wrong,
But what did I do?
Can I get a redo?
Wait, what did I do?
How can I go on?
If I don't know where or when
I went wrong?
I guess life does go on.

In My Realm of Loneliness

In my realm of loneliness,
I feel alive and free,
Pondering my thoughts,
My hopes, and dreams.
Yet I still strive
To find peace of mind,
Knowing loneliness is so unkind.

I Cry Inside

I cry inside.
It feels like I might die inside.
But I try to keep it inside
For fear of losing control.
I feel trapped in a hole.
Yes, I cry inside.

Uncertain Future

Who knows?
No one knows
But the man upstairs
What the future holds.
Just stay on your toes.
The future is untold.

My Bed

My bed is
Already made
By no maid.
With very little shade,
All I can do is lie
In the bed that is
Already made
And some hope for
Some aid.

My Prayer

I pray
Each and every day
Before I lie.
Sometimes I replay
And wish
I could just get away.
But I'm here to stay.
So, I pray
My story will lay
Before my last day.

Love Is One of a Kind

As I write this
To you,
My heart is true.
Without your love,
I feel blue.
You are constantly in my mind.
I thank God you are mine.
Your love is one of a kind
And hard to find.

Life Is a Book

Life is a book
With many chapters
And many beginnings.
So, take a look
To see
What road I took
That made my book.

An End of an Era

The end of a chapter
Marks the beginning
Of a new chapter,
A rebirth.
Just remember you are the author
And the narrator of
An end of an era.

It's Me

Open your eyes
To see
It's just me.
Please don't flee.
It's me.
Just let me be,
And you will see
The beauty
Within me.

Scares of Sorrow

Scares full of sorrow,
How I wish it were tomorrow.
But everywhere I go,
These scares are sure to follow.
So I just have to swallow
My scares of sorrow.

Remember Me

Remember me.
Remember my name.
Remember I came,
Not for all the fame,
But to take aim
And win my game.
That's what I claim.

A Call to All Chicanos

I'm fed up.
Chicanos need to wake up.
We need to shape up
And raise up
To shake things up.
And don't let up
Until we all get up.
And never give up
Before we come up.

To All My Readers

I write to you.
This is for all of you.
Hopefully to inspire you
And light a fire within you
To reach for what you desire,
Like those you admire.

God Bless the Dead

Before I go to bed
To rest my head,
So many tears we shed.
I ask God
To bless the dead
And for them to rest in peace.

Your Voice

Let your voice be known.
Don't just moan
And groan.
Give your voice a strong tone
So, you won't feel all alone.
Use your voice;
It's your voice.

Life Is a Risk

Nothing is for sure,
Only that death will occur.
So, rest assured
In what you prefer
And in what you defer.
Remember, you are
Your own chauffeur,
And life is a risk.

Those We Loved and Lost, RIP

To those who died,
What a noble price to pay.
The cost to be idolized.
Their graves become our altars.
Their memorials are our mourning,
Which we express and glorify.
But their fates we admire
With a burning fire
That we desire.

Thank You, Mom

Thank you for all you do.
Especially when I felt blue,
In my darkest moments and yours too.
I knew I could always count on you
To make me remain true.
For that I will always be in debt to you.
Of course, I love you.
Thank you.

My Time to Shine

Is it my time to shine?
Through all the trials and tribulations
Of life, it makes me ask
When is it my time to shine?
I guess these obstacles test you
And prepare you for what's next.
One must seize the opportunity
To make every moment count.
Everyone has a time.
Yes, this is my mine,
It is my time to shine.

Origel

This is my surname.
Wow, look how far we came
And how many obstacles we overcame,
Even before I came.
It was unknown to shame
And unable to tame
This name,
Which, with honor and pride,
I claim
To have the surname of Origel.

Many Mountains to Climb

Many mountains to climb.
Too many to count.
Nothing but time.
Look how far I've fallen behind.
Makes me feel like I should run and hide.
But I must stay and fight
Until I see the light.
Lord knows I try with all my might
To stay right
And follow the light.
But why must they be so tight.
I know one day it will be all right.

My Birth

My birth was not plain.
It was full of pain.
Hard to restrain
All the pain.
Even then only a few remained
To witness what was gained
At my birth.

I'm Here

Hello, I'm here.
No need to fear.
See me as a mirror.
I'll even let you use my ear.
Hopefully, you will learn to cheer
Since I'm near.
Yes, I'm right here.
I've been here,
And I'm still here.
Thank God I'm here.

Book of a Dream

This is a book of a dream
Of a bigger scheme
That has the important theme
Of helping others achieve their own dreams,
Like a beam
With a team,
I was able to achieve my dream.

Family Tree

I come from a family of inspirational people.
As I dig deeper
And deeper,
I find so many inspirational people.
I feel so amazed
And a bit dazed
But yet honored
To be around such great people.

In My Shell

I'm in my shell.
My comfortable hell.
I want to scream
And yell
But to no avail.
I feel trapped in my shell.
But who can tell?
If I'm always in my shell?

The Hourglass

My life is like an hourglass.
As I look at the hourglass,
I think about the past
And my next task.
I wonder if I'm still blinded
By the same mask
From my past.
Should I dash
Before the last
Of the hourglass?

Power of Desire

My power of desire
Burns like fire.
Higher and higher
Until I'm in dire need
To lead by my willpower
In whatever I desire.
That's my power of desire.

The Thoughts of a Crazy Individual

The thoughts in my head are like bullets of a loaded gun, traveling at a fast Pace.
My thoughts overwhelm me with a ton of emotions.
My heart fills with devotion.
But no one can fully understand
All the crazy thoughts going through my mind.
My thoughts travel in my brain at the speed of light.
These are the thoughts of a crazy individual.

Revolutionaries of the Past

I desire to have my
Views and visions of the future
To out last
My life's final task
But, is this my true task?
I ask
To reveal the mask
Which covers our horrible past
Like the revolutionaries of the past
Change is still needed
To see the world
Clear as glass
And mend our broken hearts
At last.

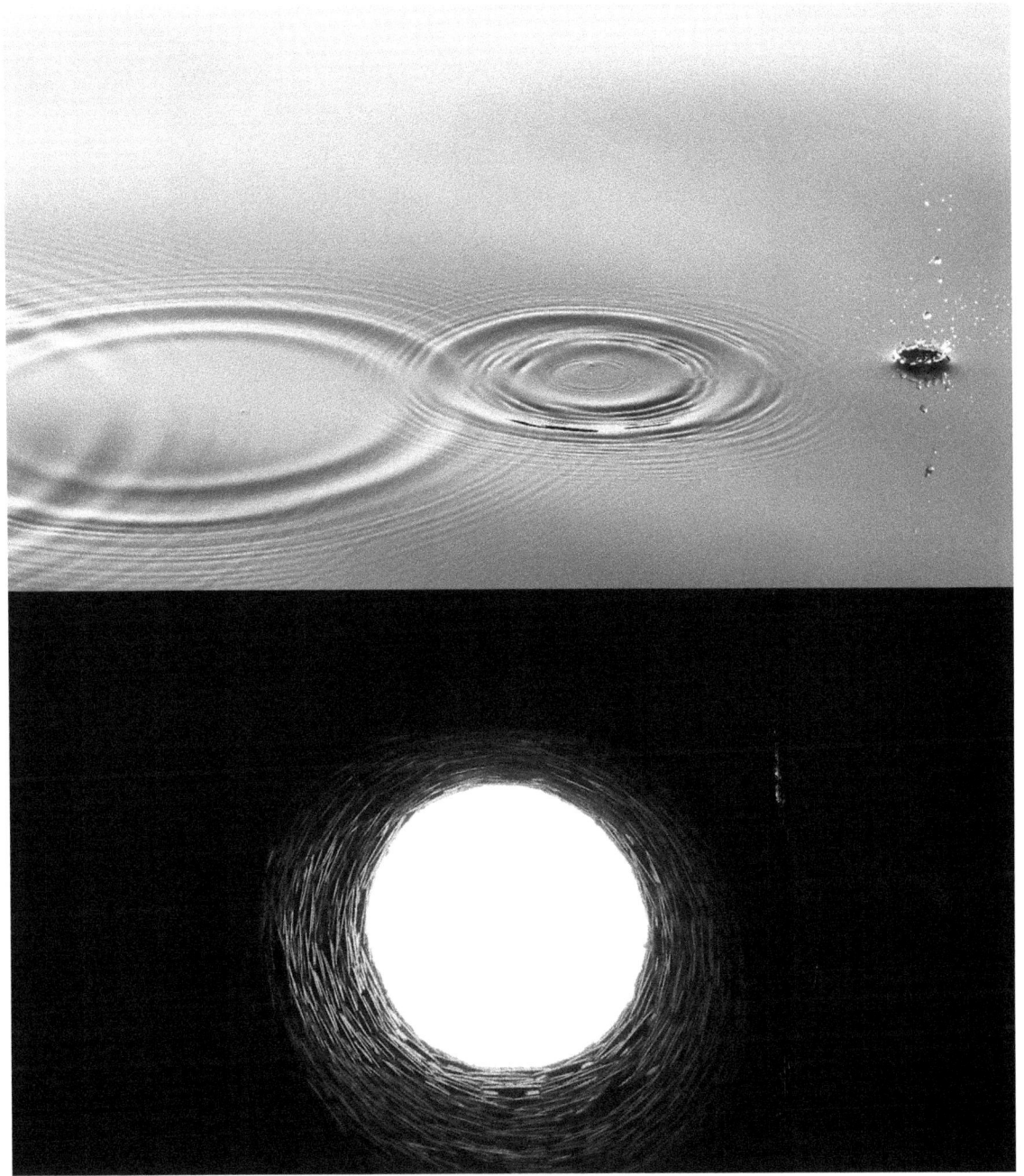

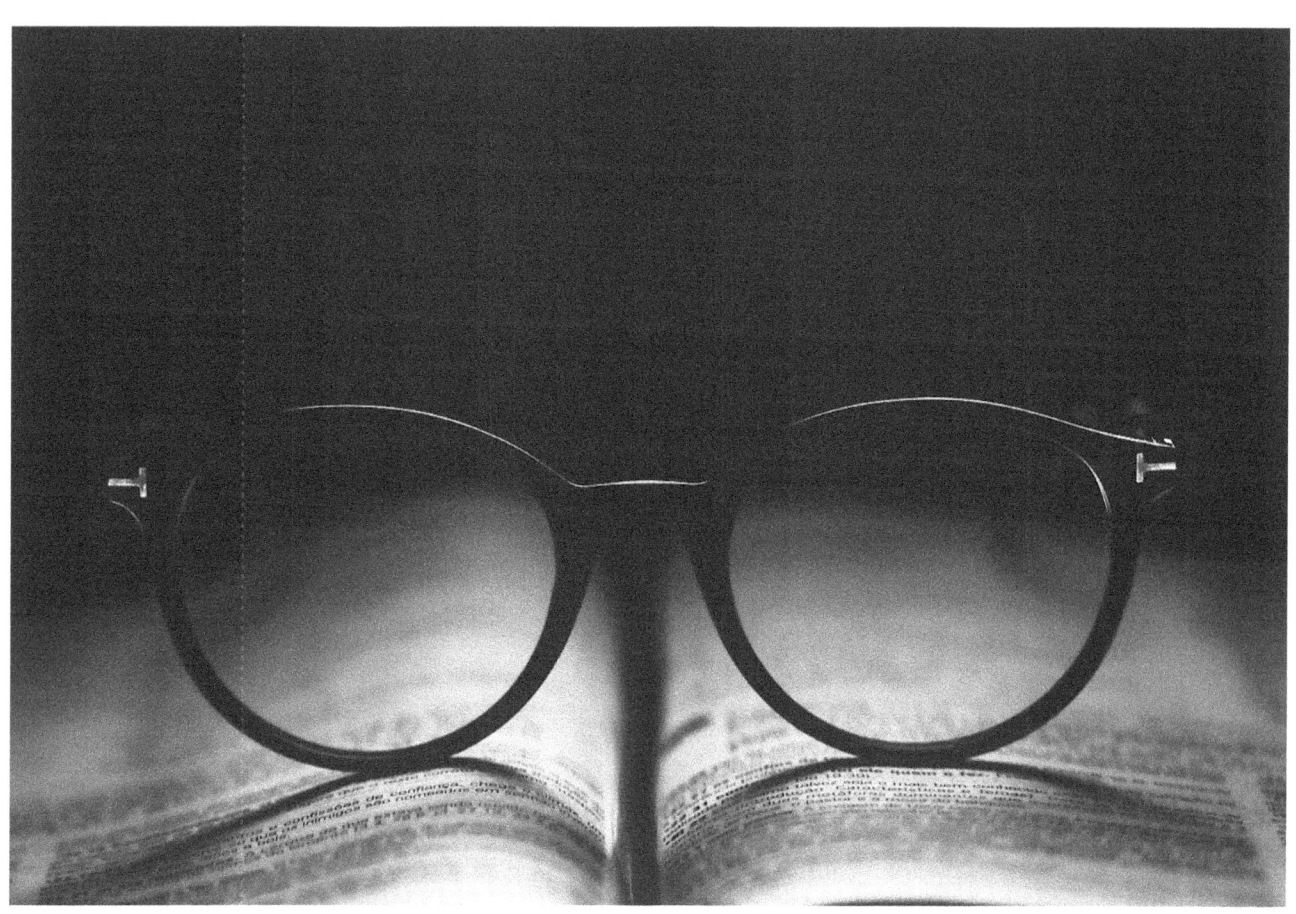

About the Author

He recently received his second associate's degree. Also accumulating of numerous certificates of Achievement and Proficiency in areas of computer studies and business. A polite and respectable young man, he has a strong work ethic and humble attitude. He is very relatable to others

About the Book

The author gives a personal account of his life in a poetic format. He gives motivational and inspirational encouragement though his writings. In this book, the author shares his thoughts and struggles throughout his life in the hope of impacting and encouraging others to reach for their goals and dreams.

www.ingramcontent.com/pod-product-compliance
Ingram Content Group UK Ltd.
Pitfield, Milton Keynes, MK11 3LW, UK
UKHW050409240426
12048UKWH00020B/1419